T0419195

TRAGEDY! TALES FROM THE TITANIC

Building the Ship of Dreams

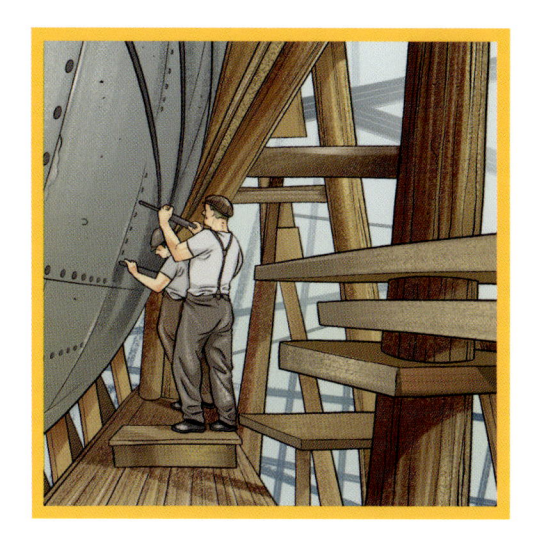

BY SARAH EASON

ILLUSTRATED BY ALEK SOTIROVSKI

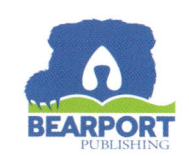

BEARPORT PUBLISHING

Minneapolis, Minnesota

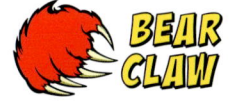

BEAR CLAW

Credits

20, © Alamy/Pictorial Press Ltd; 21t, © Wikimedia Commons/Robert Welch; 21b, © Shutterstock/Kit Leong; 22t, © Shutterstock/Meunierd; 22b, © Wikimedia Commons; 23, © Wikimedia Commons/Robert Welch.

Editor: Jennifer Sanderson
Proofreader: Katie Dicker
Designer: Paul Myerscough
Picture Researcher: Katie Dicker

Bearport Publishing Company Product Development Team
Publisher: Jen Jenson; Director of Product Development: Spencer Brinker; Managing Editor: Allison Juda; Editor: Cole Nelson; Associate Editor: Naomi Reich; Associate Editor: Tiana Tran; Art Director: Colin O'Dea; Designer: Kim Jones; Designer: Kayla Eggert; Product Development Specialist: Owen Hamlin

Statement on Usage of Generative Artificial Intelligence
Bearport Publishing remains committed to publishing high-quality nonfiction books. Therefore, we restrict the use of generative AI to ensure accuracy of all text and visual components pertaining to a book's subject. See BearportPublishing.com for details.

A Note on Graphic Narrative Nonfiction
This graphic story is a dramatization based on true events. It is intended to give the reader a sense of the narrative rather than a presentation of actual details as they occurred.

Library of Congress Cataloging-in-Publication Data

Names: Eason, Sarah, author. | Sotirovski, Aleksandar, illustrator.
Title: Building the ship of dreams / by Sarah Eason ; illustrated by Alek Sotirovski.
Description: Bear claw books. | Minneapolis, Minnesota : Bearport Publishing, [2025] | Series: Tragedy! Tales from the Titanic | Bear claw books. | Includes bibliographical references and index.
Identifiers: LCCN 2024034190 (print) | LCCN 2024034191 (ebook) | ISBN 9798892328548 (library binding) | ISBN 9798892329446 (paperback) | ISBN 9798892328616 (ebook)
Subjects: LCSH: Titanic (Steamship)--Design and construction--Juvenile literature. | Titanic (Steamship)--Design and construction--Comic books, strips, etc.
Classification: LCC VM383.T57 E37 2025 (print) | LCC VM383.T57 (ebook) | DDC 623.82/432--dc23/eng/20240809
LC record available at https://lccn.loc.gov/2024034190
LC ebook record available at https://lccn.loc.gov/2024034191

Copyright © 2025 Bearport Publishing Company. All rights reserved. No part of this publication may be reproduced in whole or in part, stored in any retrieval system, or transmitted in any form or by any means, electronic, mechanical, photocopying, recording, or otherwise, without written permission from the publisher.

For more information, write to Bearport Publishing, 5357 Penn Avenue South, Minneapolis, MN 55419.

Contents

CHAPTER 1

Ship of Dreams

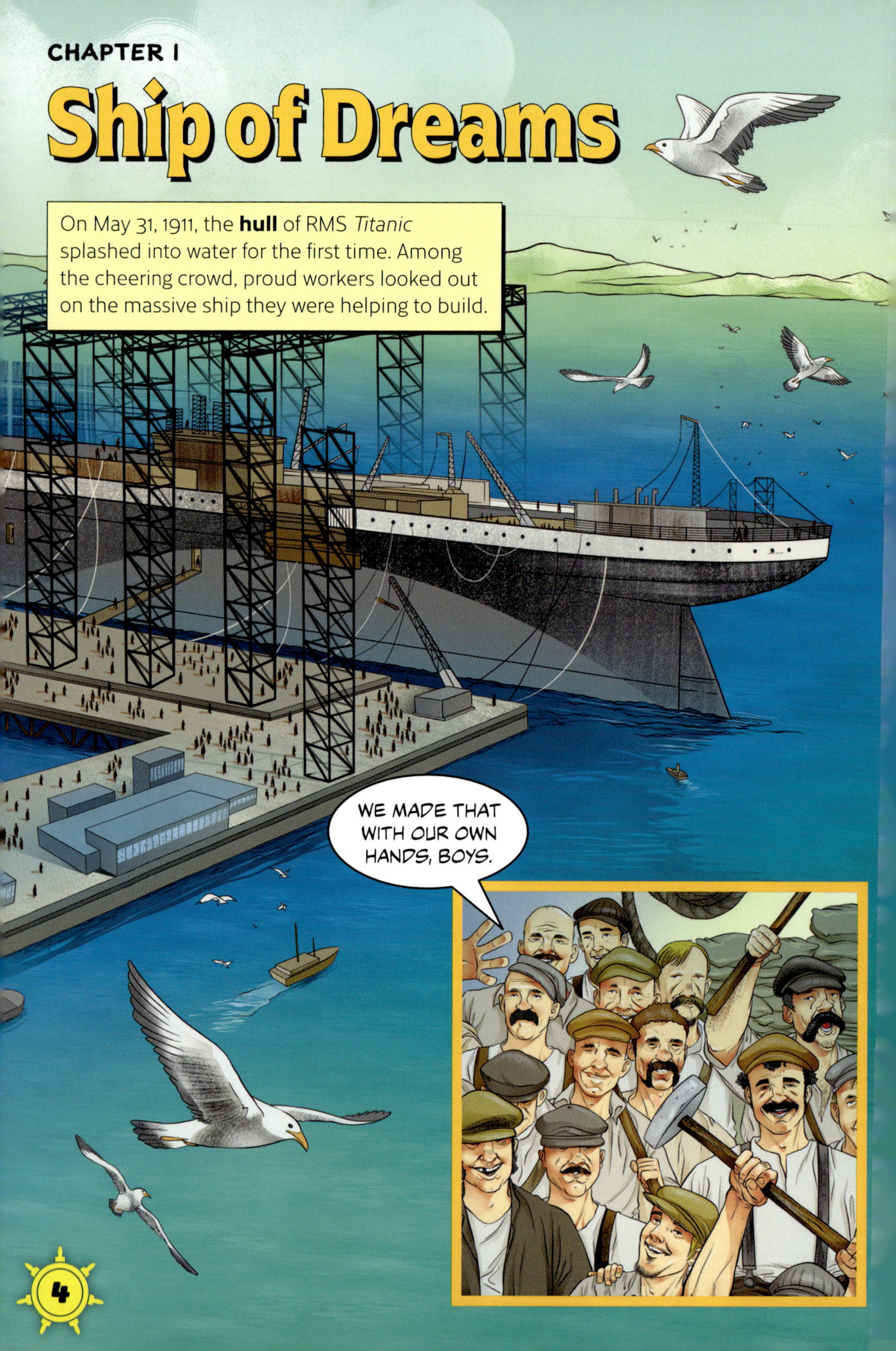
On May 31, 1911, the **hull** of RMS *Titanic* splashed into water for the first time. Among the cheering crowd, proud workers looked out on the massive ship they were helping to build.
WE MADE THAT WITH OUR OWN HANDS, BOYS.

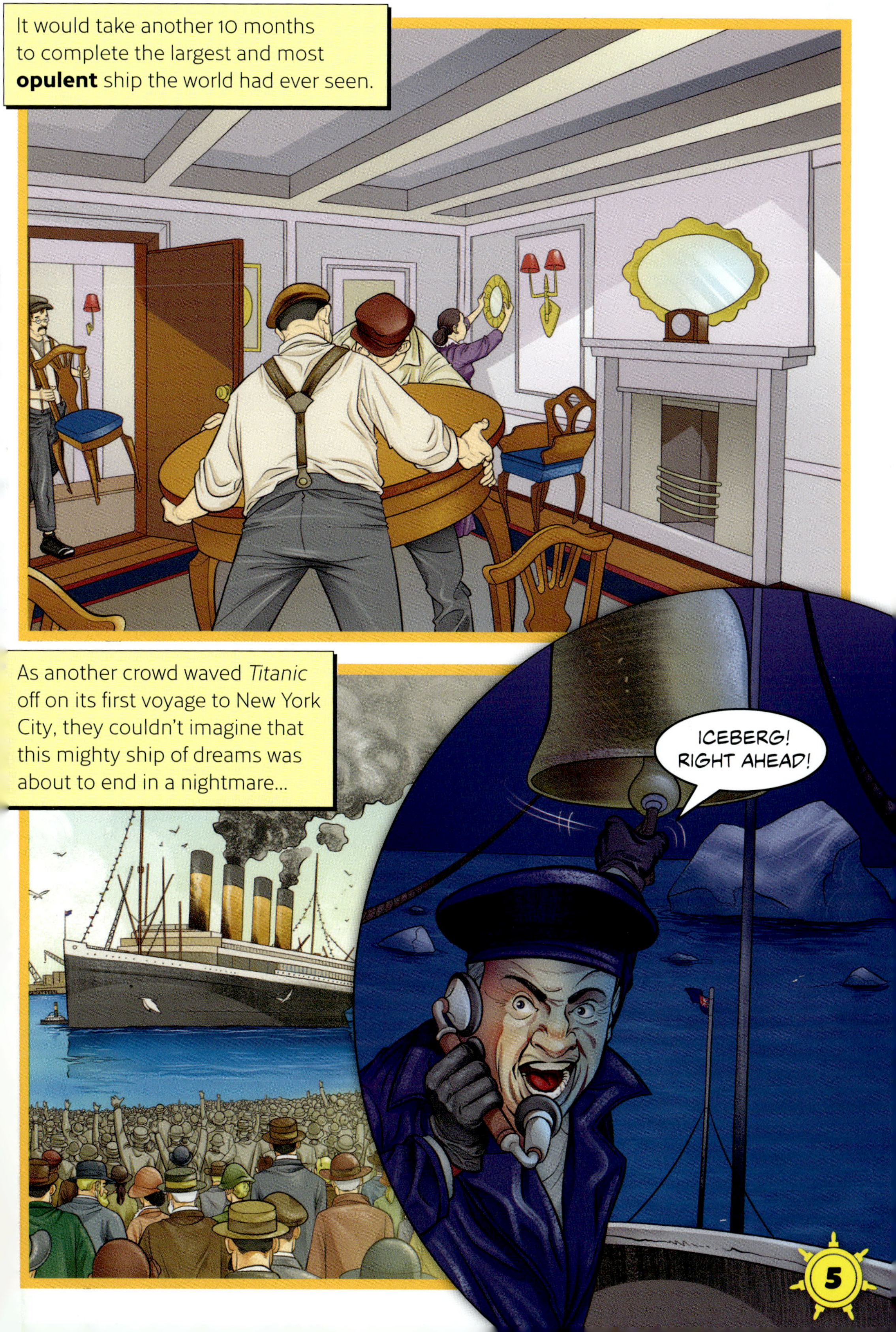
It would take another 10 months to complete the largest and most **opulent** ship the world had ever seen.
As another crowd waved *Titanic* off on its first voyage to New York City, they couldn't imagine that this mighty ship of dreams was about to end in a nightmare...
ICEBERG! RIGHT AHEAD!

CHAPTER 2

Big Plans

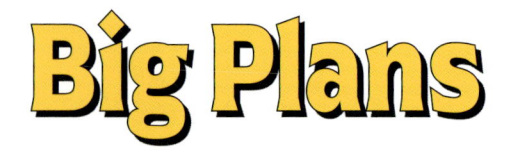

In the early 1900s, the fastest way to travel across the Atlantic Ocean was on a steamship. Demand for large steamships was growing.

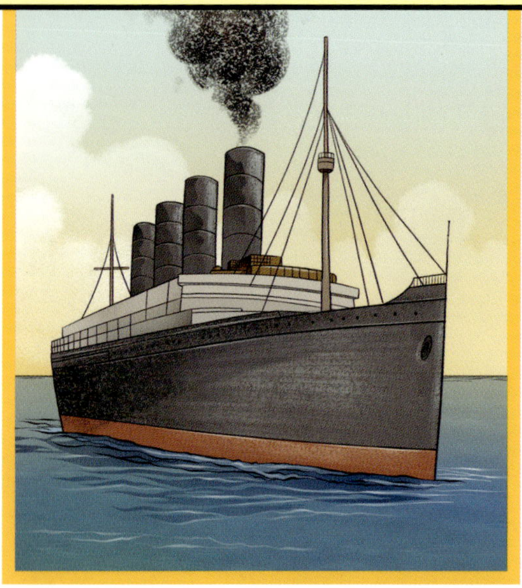

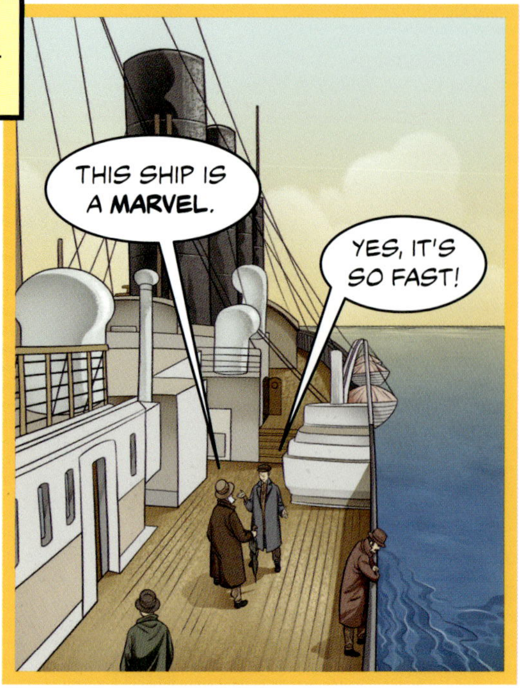
THIS SHIP IS A **MARVEL**.
YES, IT'S SO FAST!

J. Bruce Ismay wanted to build a group of ships known for both comfort and speed.

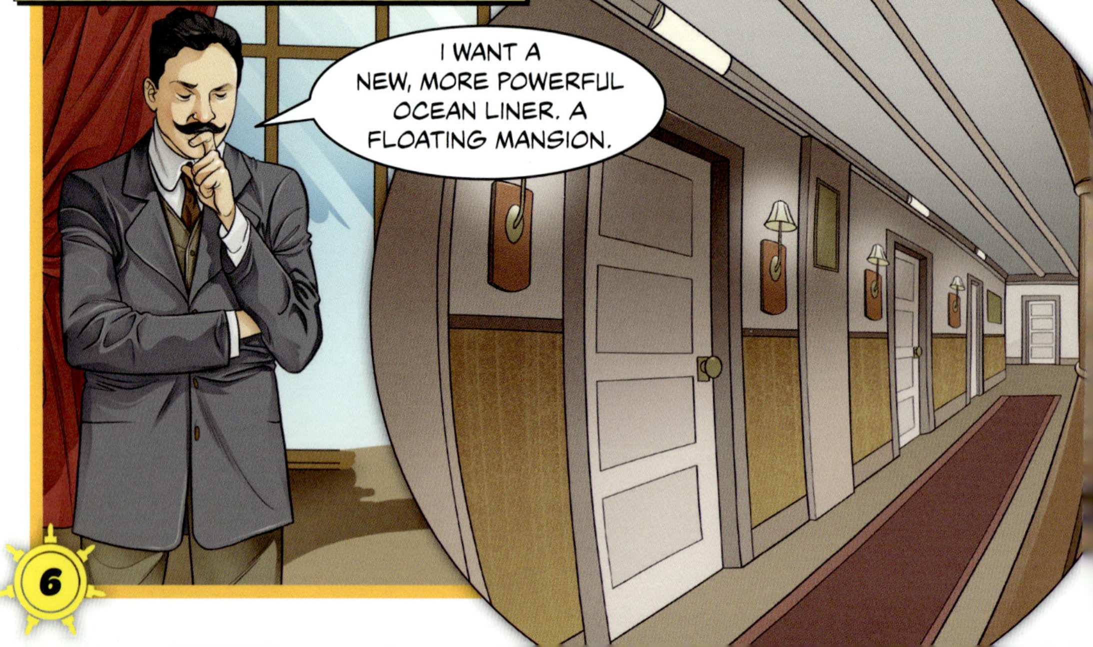
I WANT A NEW, MORE POWERFUL OCEAN LINER. A FLOATING MANSION.

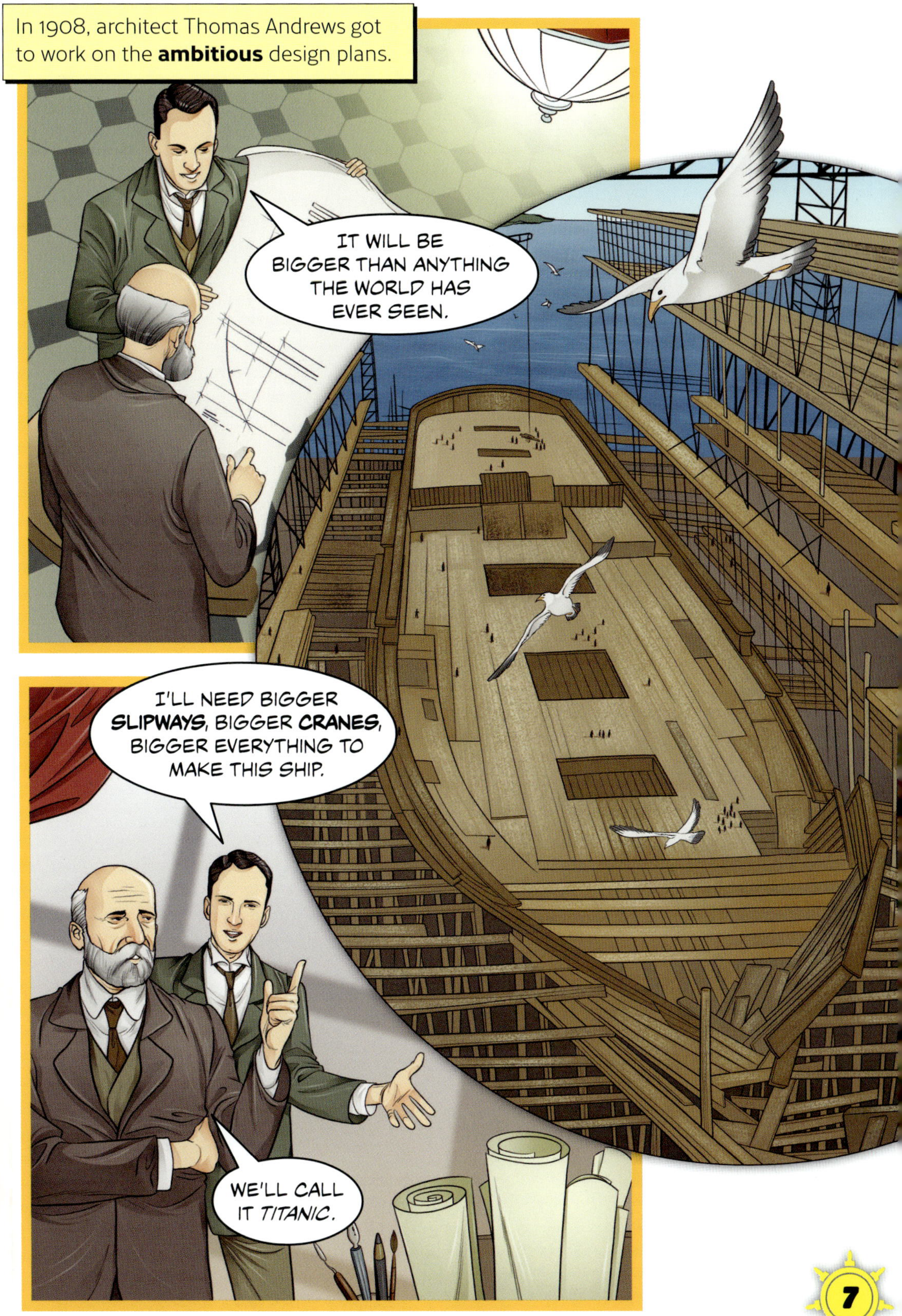
In 1908, architect Thomas Andrews got to work on the **ambitious** design plans.
IT WILL BE BIGGER THAN ANYTHING THE WORLD HAS EVER SEEN.
I'LL NEED BIGGER **SLIPWAYS**, BIGGER **CRANES**, BIGGER EVERYTHING TO MAKE THIS SHIP.
WE'LL CALL IT *TITANIC*.

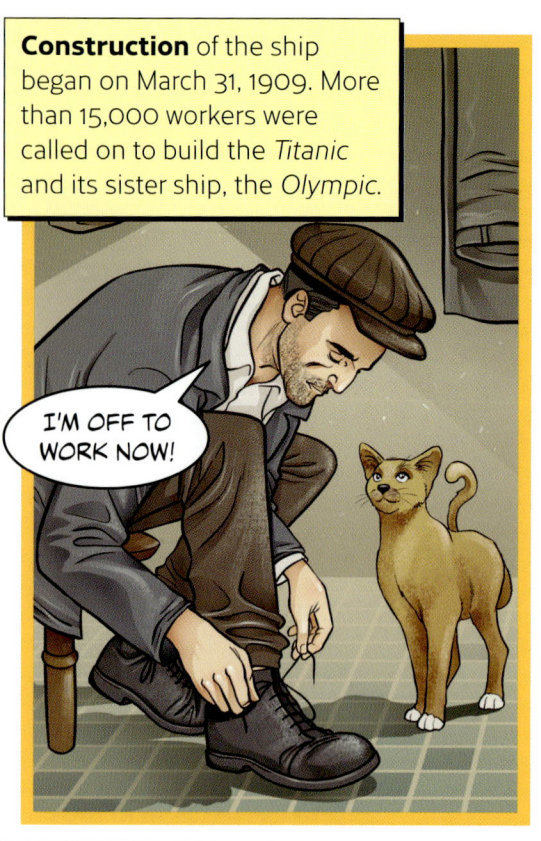

Construction of the ship began on March 31, 1909. More than 15,000 workers were called on to build the *Titanic* and its sister ship, the *Olympic*.

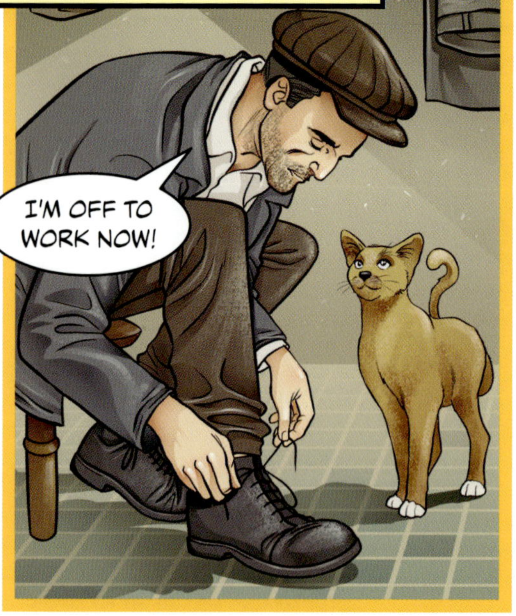
I'M OFF TO WORK NOW!

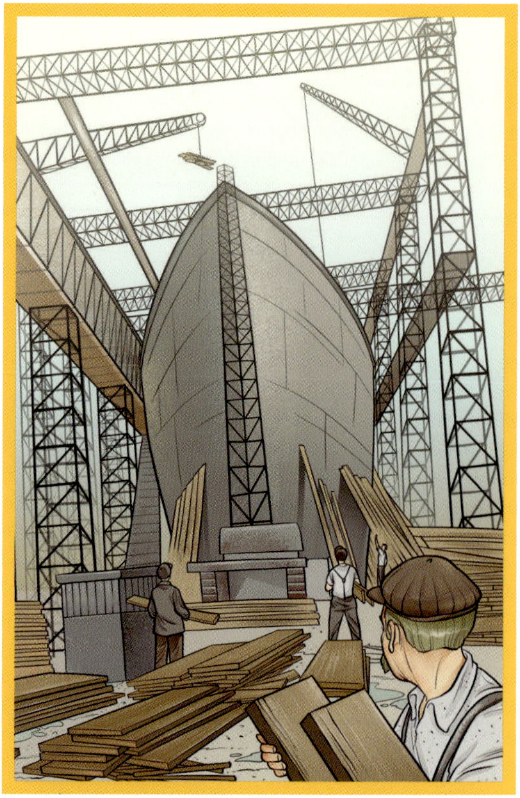

Teams of **carpenters**, electricians, dockworkers, and **riveters** all played important roles.

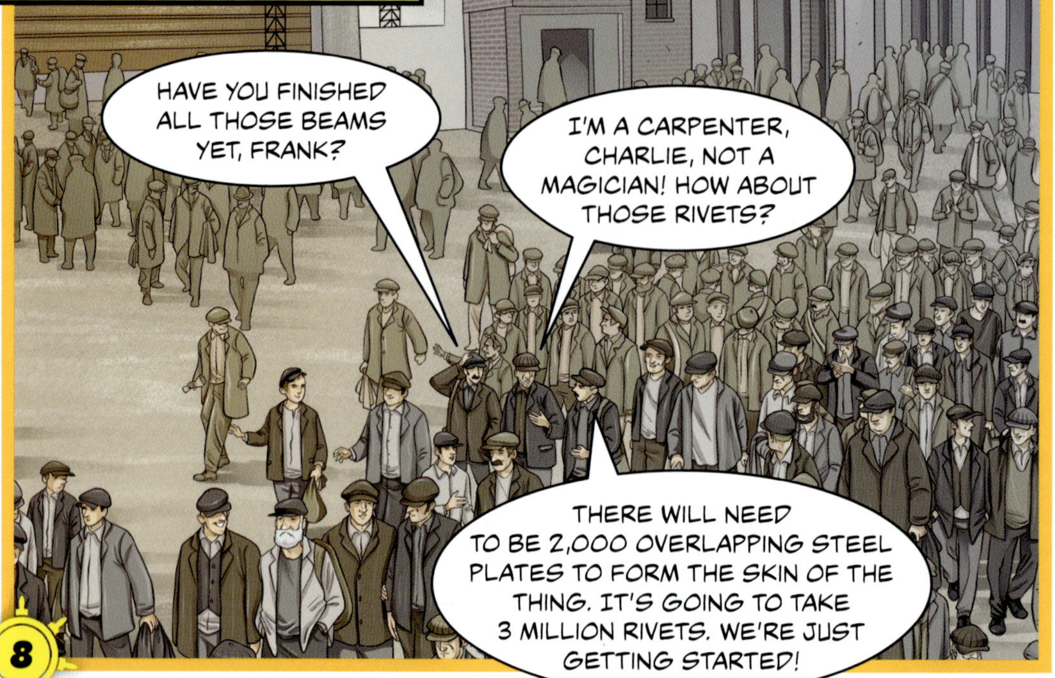
HAVE YOU FINISHED ALL THOSE BEAMS YET, FRANK?
I'M A CARPENTER, CHARLIE, NOT A MAGICIAN! HOW ABOUT THOSE RIVETS?
THERE WILL NEED TO BE 2,000 OVERLAPPING STEEL PLATES TO FORM THE SKIN OF THE THING. IT'S GOING TO TAKE 3 MILLION RIVETS. WE'RE JUST GETTING STARTED!

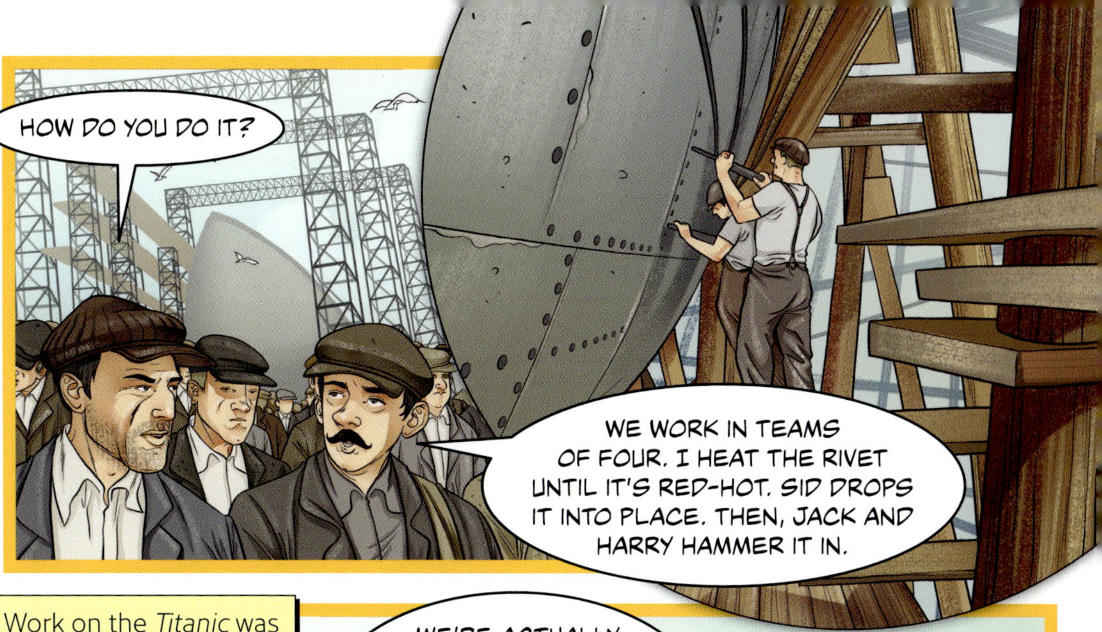
HOW DO YOU DO IT?
WE WORK IN TEAMS OF FOUR. I HEAT THE RIVET UNTIL IT'S RED-HOT. SID DROPS IT INTO PLACE. THEN, JACK AND HARRY HAMMER IT IN.

Work on the *Titanic* was not always easy. Plenty of workers got hurt.

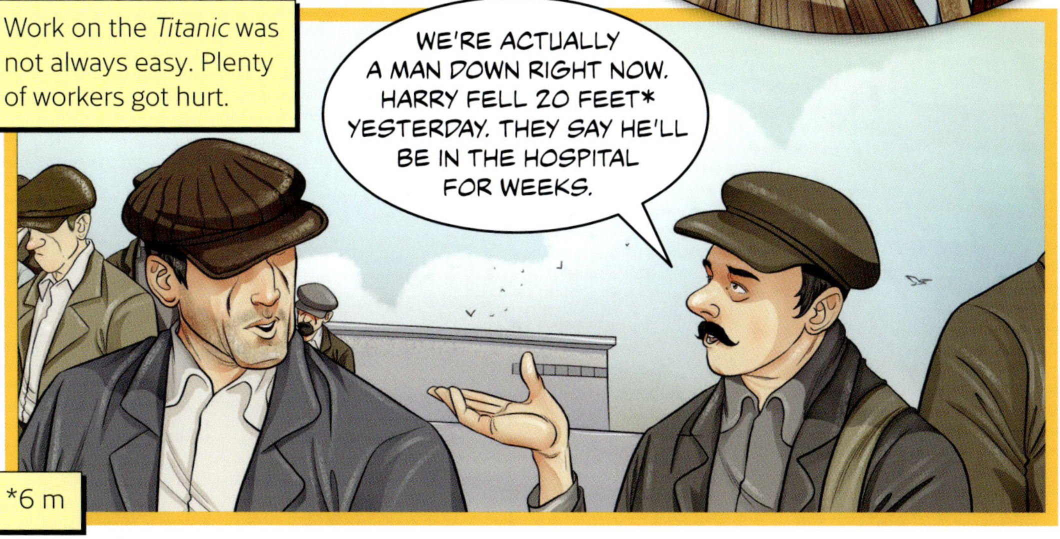
WE'RE ACTUALLY A MAN DOWN RIGHT NOW. HARRY FELL 20 FEET* YESTERDAY. THEY SAY HE'LL BE IN THE HOSPITAL FOR WEEKS.

*6 m

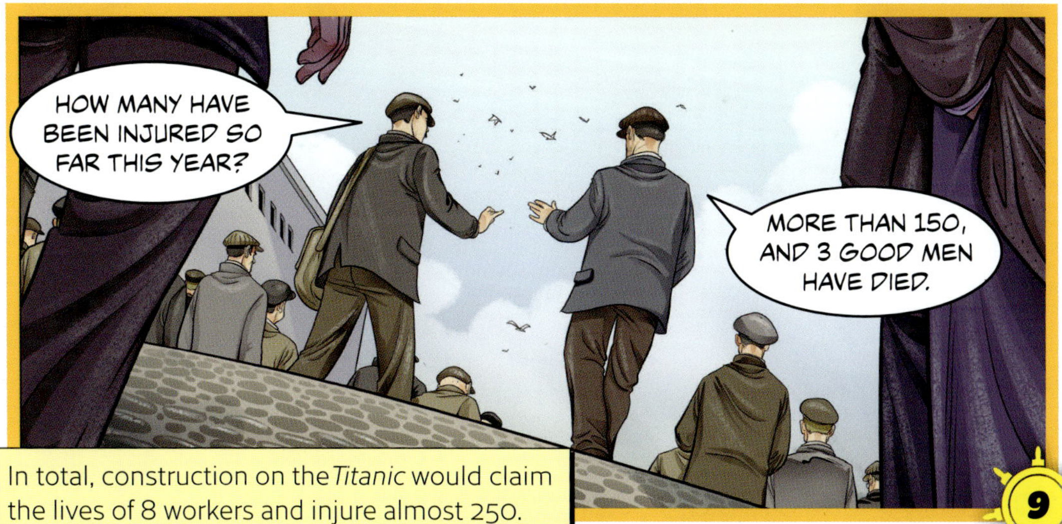
HOW MANY HAVE BEEN INJURED SO FAR THIS YEAR?
MORE THAN 150, AND 3 GOOD MEN HAVE DIED.

In total, construction on the *Titanic* would claim the lives of 8 workers and injure almost 250.

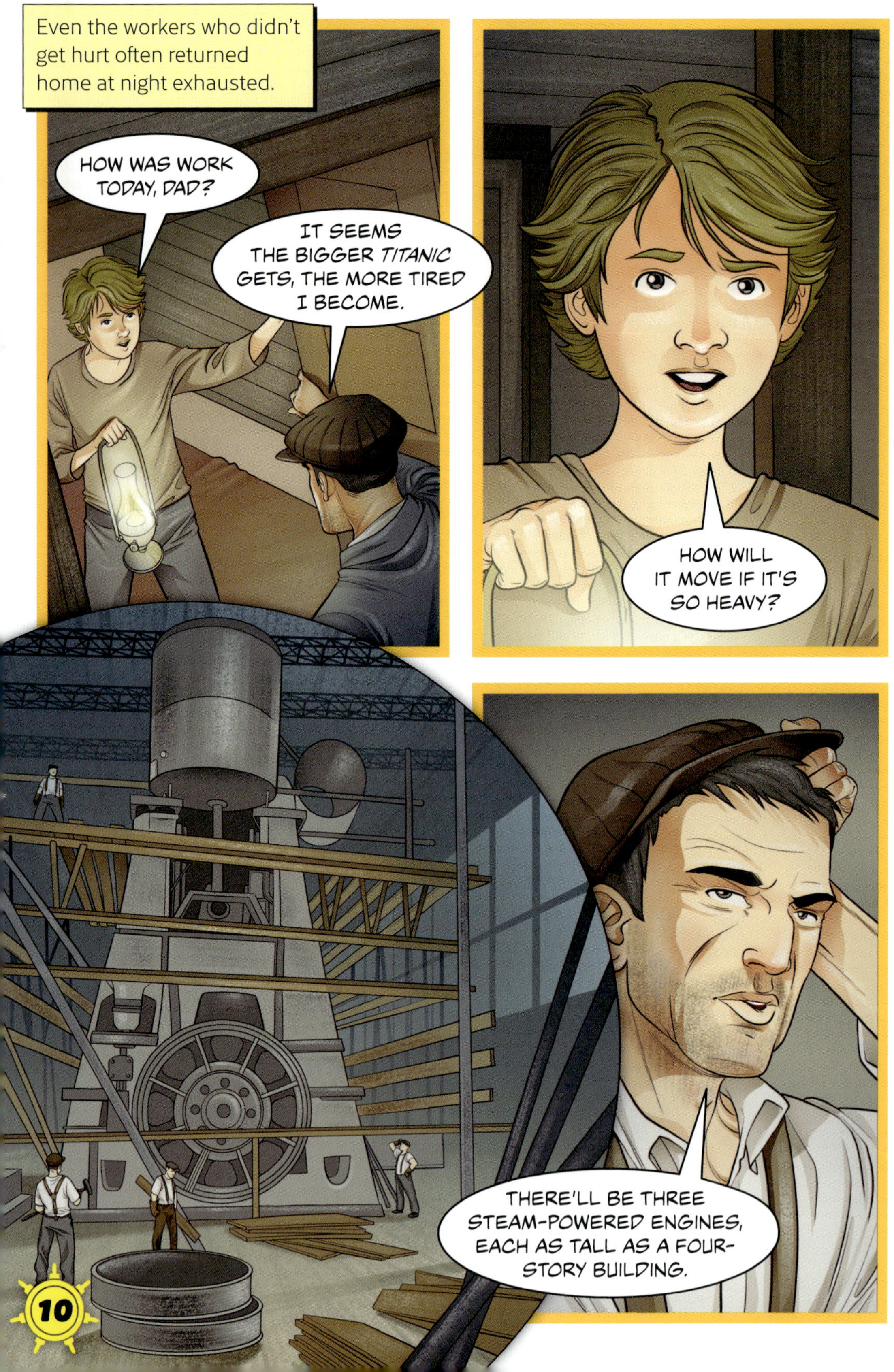
Even the workers who didn't get hurt often returned home at night exhausted.
HOW WAS WORK TODAY, DAD?
IT SEEMS THE BIGGER TITANIC GETS, THE MORE TIRED I BECOME.
HOW WILL IT MOVE IF IT'S SO HEAVY?
THERE'LL BE THREE STEAM-POWERED ENGINES, EACH AS TALL AS A FOUR-STORY BUILDING.

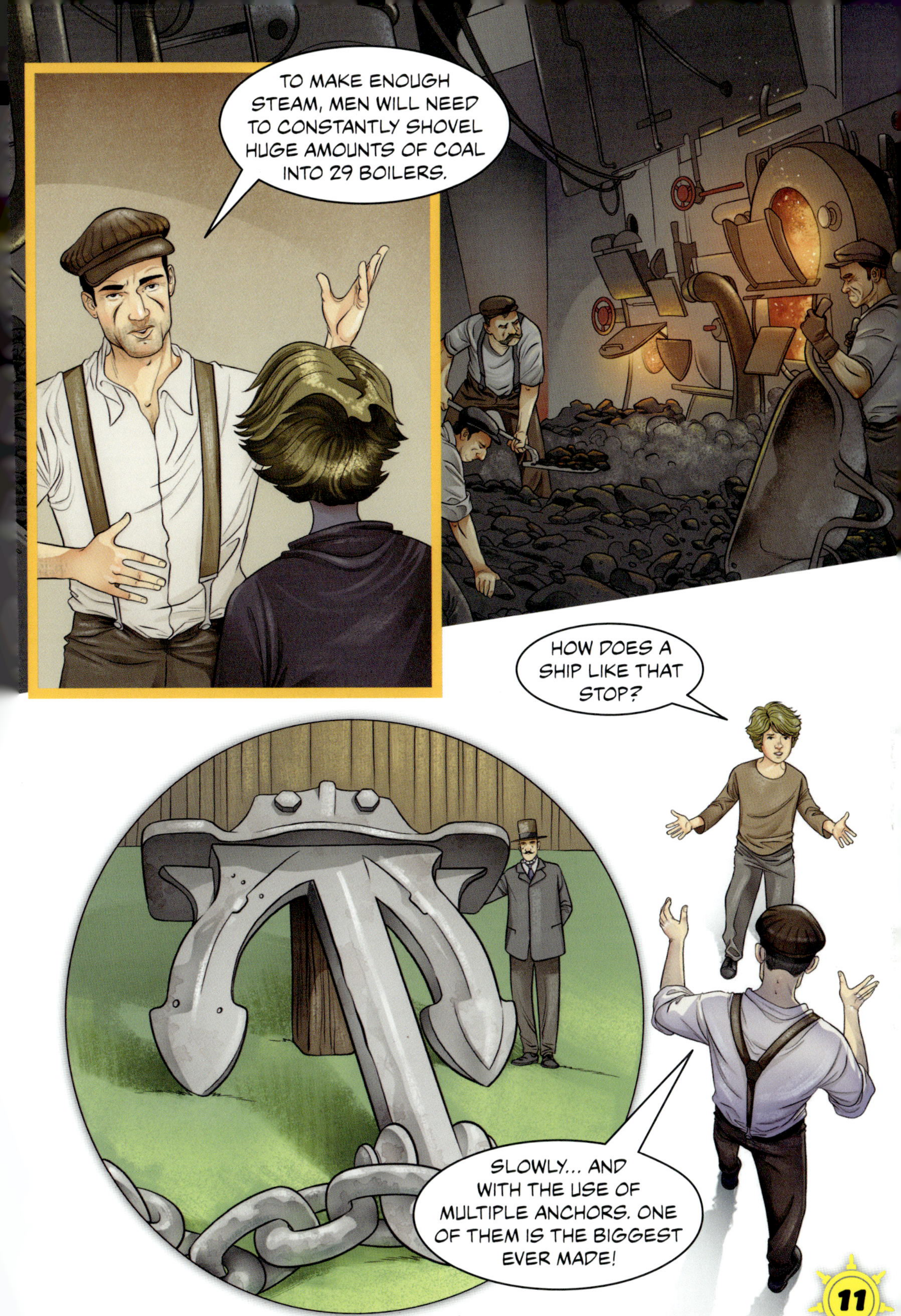
TO MAKE ENOUGH STEAM, MEN WILL NEED TO CONSTANTLY SHOVEL HUGE AMOUNTS OF COAL INTO 29 BOILERS.
HOW DOES A SHIP LIKE THAT STOP?
SLOWLY... AND WITH THE USE OF MULTIPLE ANCHORS. ONE OF THEM IS THE BIGGEST EVER MADE!

CHAPTER 3

Important Decisions

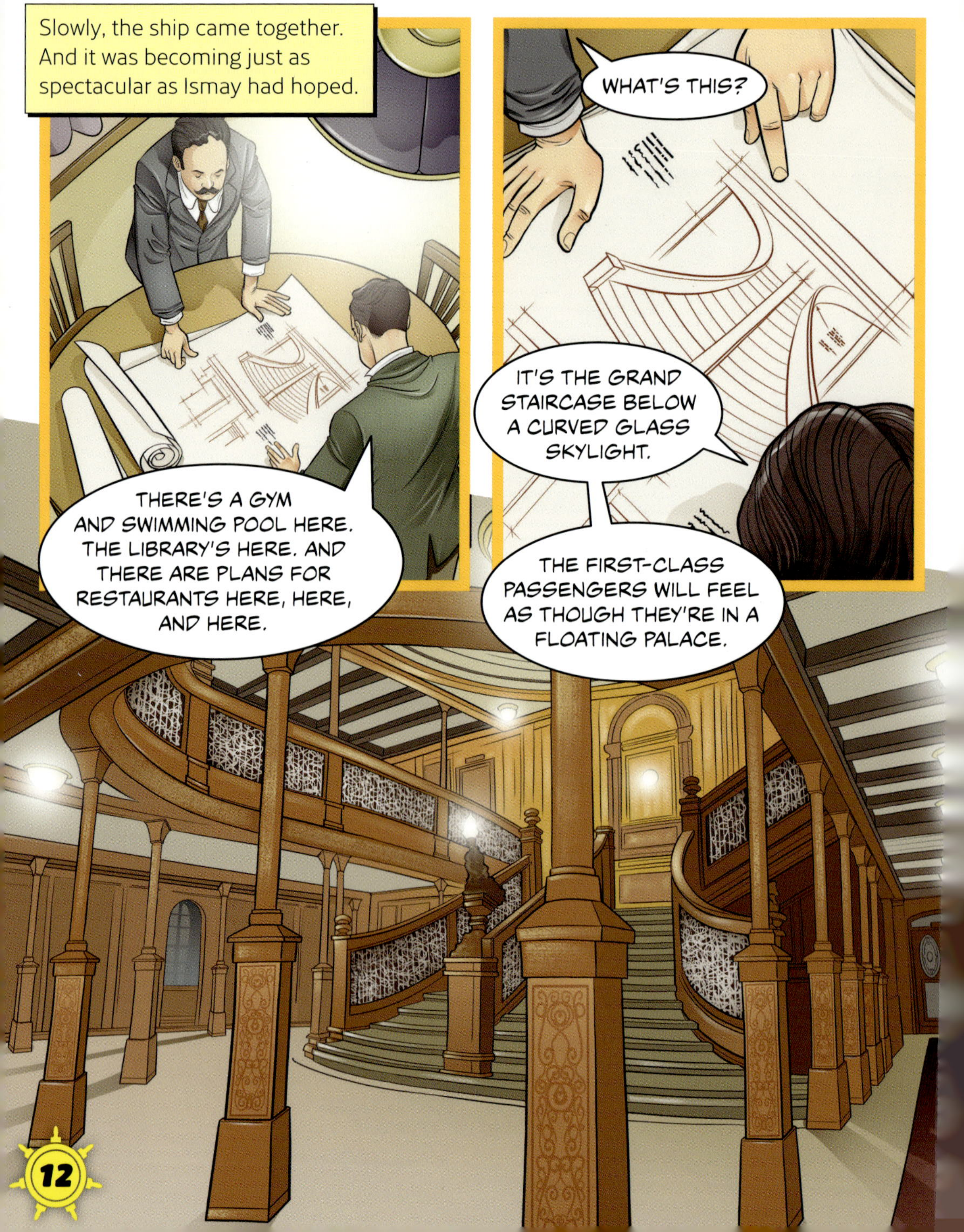
Slowly, the ship came together. And it was becoming just as spectacular as Ismay had hoped.
THERE'S A GYM AND SWIMMING POOL HERE. THE LIBRARY'S HERE. AND THERE ARE PLANS FOR RESTAURANTS HERE, HERE, AND HERE.
WHAT'S THIS?
IT'S THE GRAND STAIRCASE BELOW A CURVED GLASS SKYLIGHT.
THE FIRST-CLASS PASSENGERS WILL FEEL AS THOUGH THEY'RE IN A FLOATING PALACE.

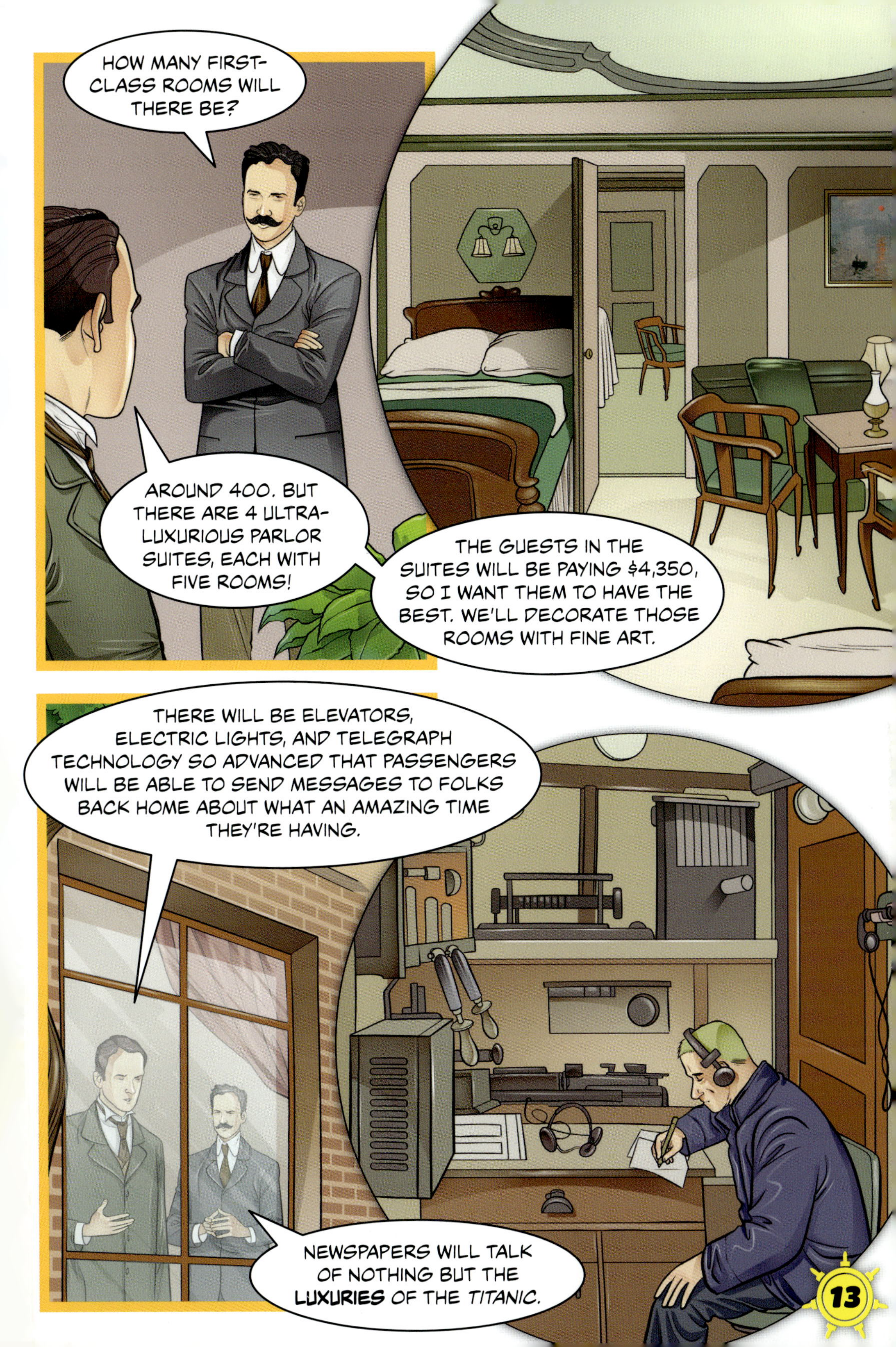
HOW MANY FIRST-CLASS ROOMS WILL THERE BE?
AROUND 400. BUT THERE ARE 4 ULTRA-LUXURIOUS PARLOR SUITES, EACH WITH FIVE ROOMS!
THE GUESTS IN THE SUITES WILL BE PAYING $4,350, SO I WANT THEM TO HAVE THE BEST. WE'LL DECORATE THOSE ROOMS WITH FINE ART.
THERE WILL BE ELEVATORS, ELECTRIC LIGHTS, AND TELEGRAPH TECHNOLOGY SO ADVANCED THAT PASSENGERS WILL BE ABLE TO SEND MESSAGES TO FOLKS BACK HOME ABOUT WHAT AN AMAZING TIME THEY'RE HAVING.
NEWSPAPERS WILL TALK OF NOTHING BUT THE **LUXURIES** OF THE *TITANIC*.

But for many passengers, life on the *Titanic* wouldn't be so glamorous.

IT'S PRETTY GLOOMY WORKING ON THE STEERAGE QUARTERS.

WHAT IS STEERAGE, FRANK?

THEY'RE THE CHEAPEST TICKETS— THIRD CLASS.

WHILE THE FIRST-CLASS PASSENGERS WILL TRAVEL IN STYLE, THERE'LL BE FOUR TO A ROOM TUCKED BELOWDECKS. AND ALL 710 STEERAGE PASSENGERS WILL HAVE TO SHARE 2 BATHTUBS.

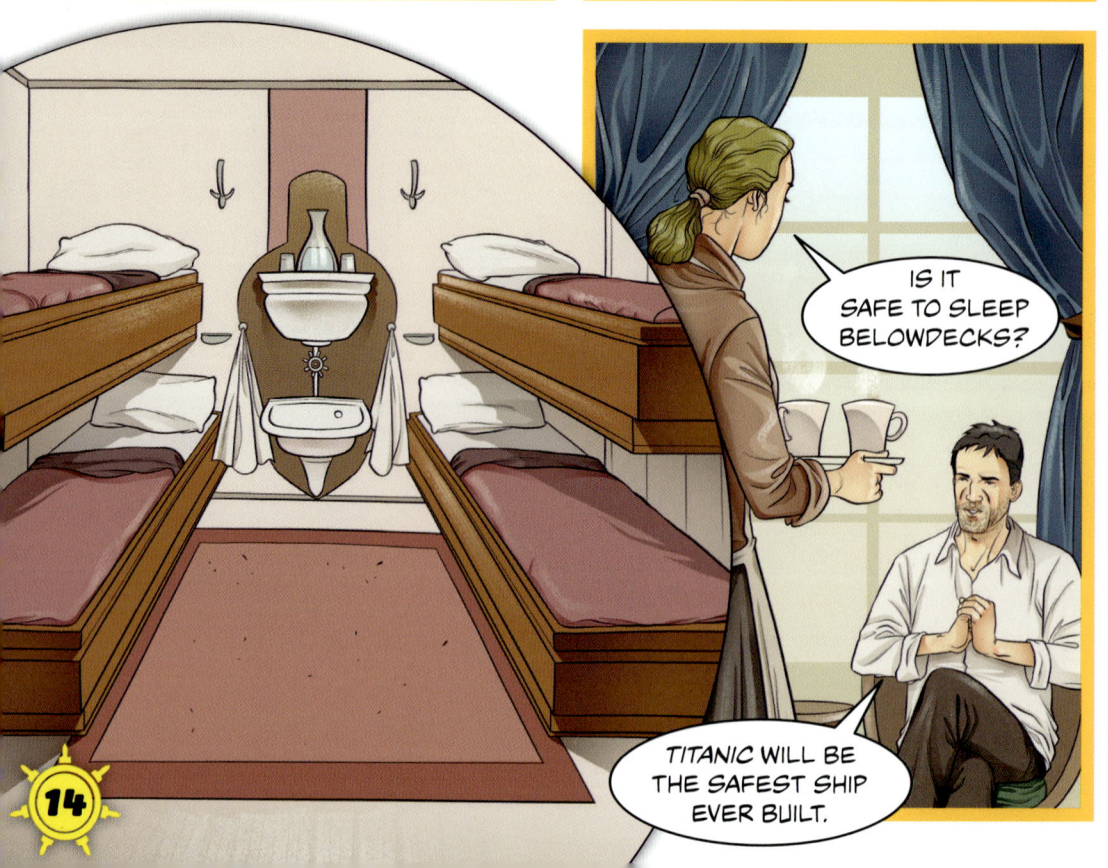

IS IT SAFE TO SLEEP BELOWDECKS?

TITANIC WILL BE THE SAFEST SHIP EVER BUILT.

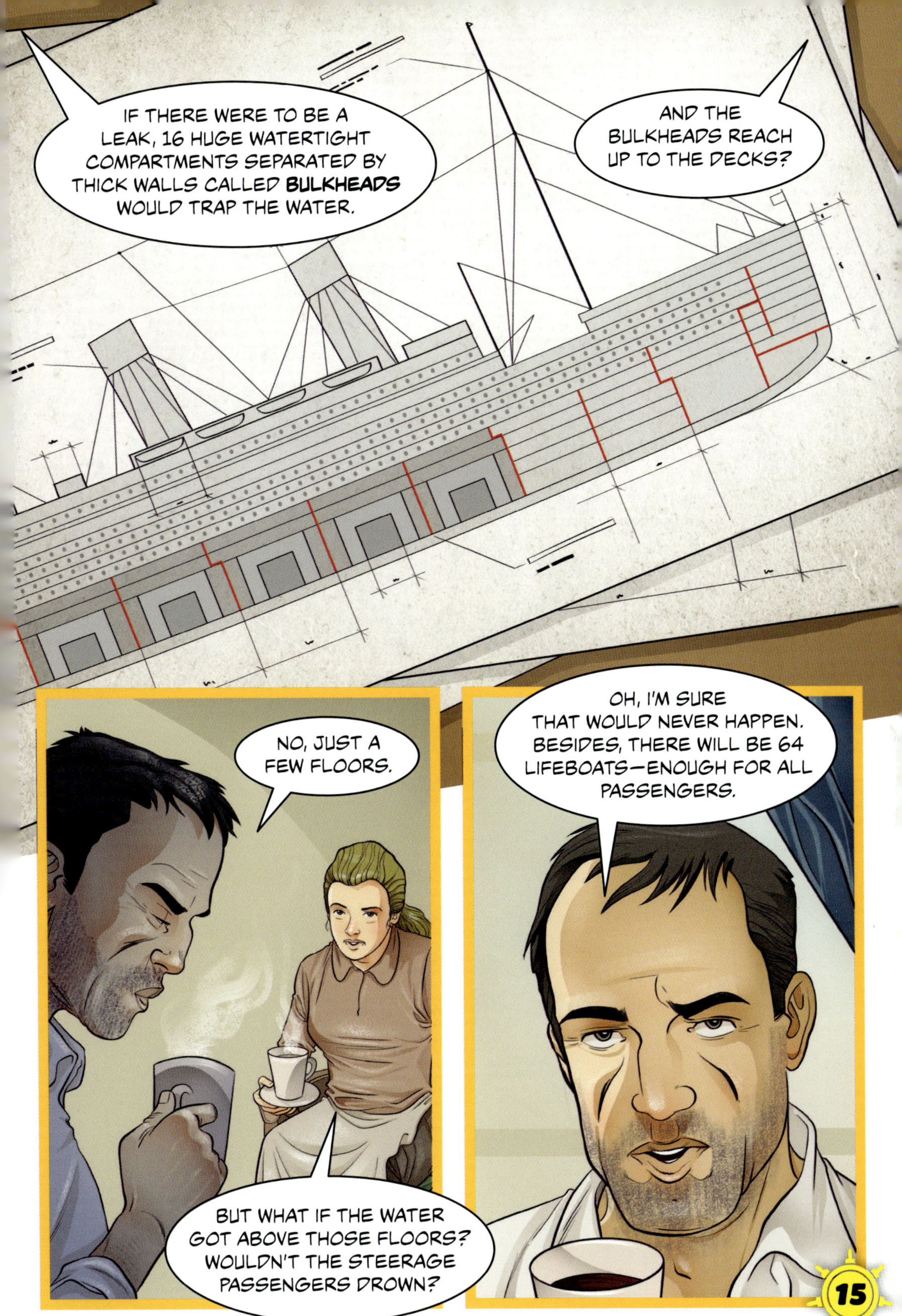
IF THERE WERE TO BE A LEAK, 16 HUGE WATERTIGHT COMPARTMENTS SEPARATED BY THICK WALLS CALLED **BULKHEADS** WOULD TRAP THE WATER.
AND THE BULKHEADS REACH UP TO THE DECKS?
NO, JUST A FEW FLOORS.
BUT WHAT IF THE WATER GOT ABOVE THOSE FLOORS? WOULDN'T THE STEERAGE PASSENGERS DROWN?
OH, I'M SURE THAT WOULD NEVER HAPPEN. BESIDES, THERE WILL BE 64 LIFEBOATS—ENOUGH FOR ALL PASSENGERS.

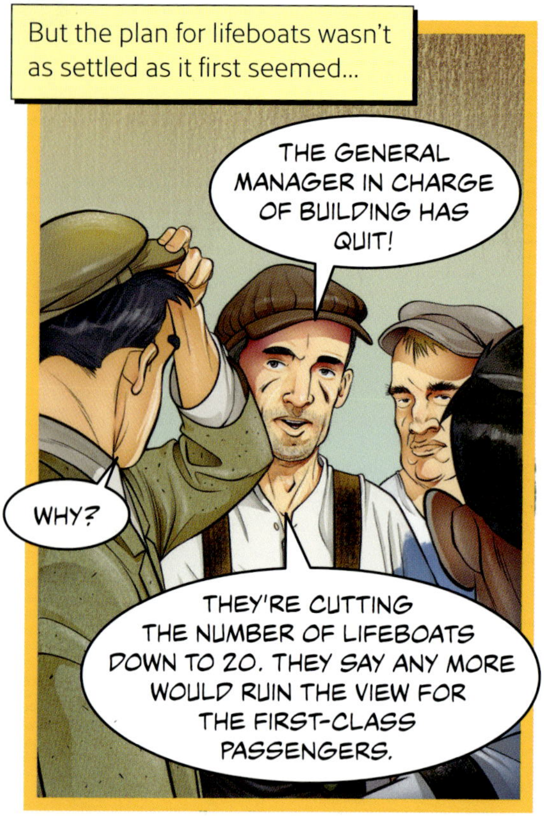
But the plan for lifeboats wasn't as settled as it first seemed...
THE GENERAL MANAGER IN CHARGE OF BUILDING HAS QUIT!
WHY?
THEY'RE CUTTING THE NUMBER OF LIFEBOATS DOWN TO 20. THEY SAY ANY MORE WOULD RUIN THE VIEW FOR THE FIRST-CLASS PASSENGERS.

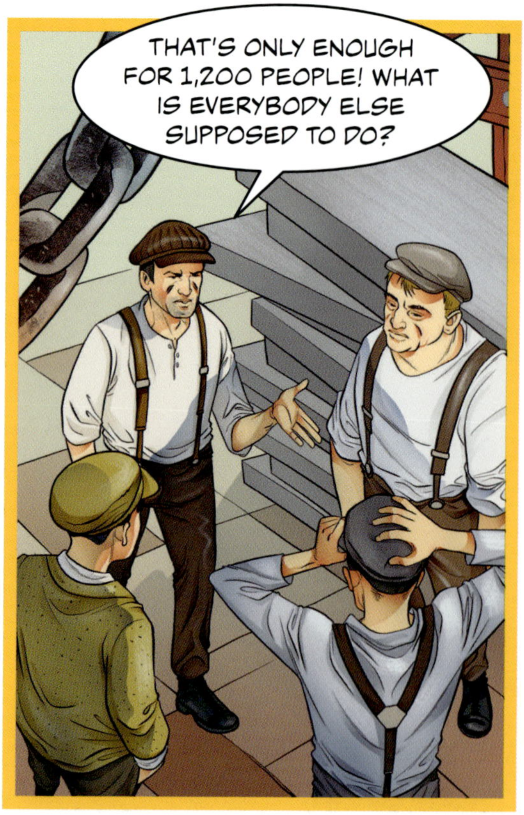
THAT'S ONLY ENOUGH FOR 1,200 PEOPLE! WHAT IS EVERYBODY ELSE SUPPOSED TO DO?

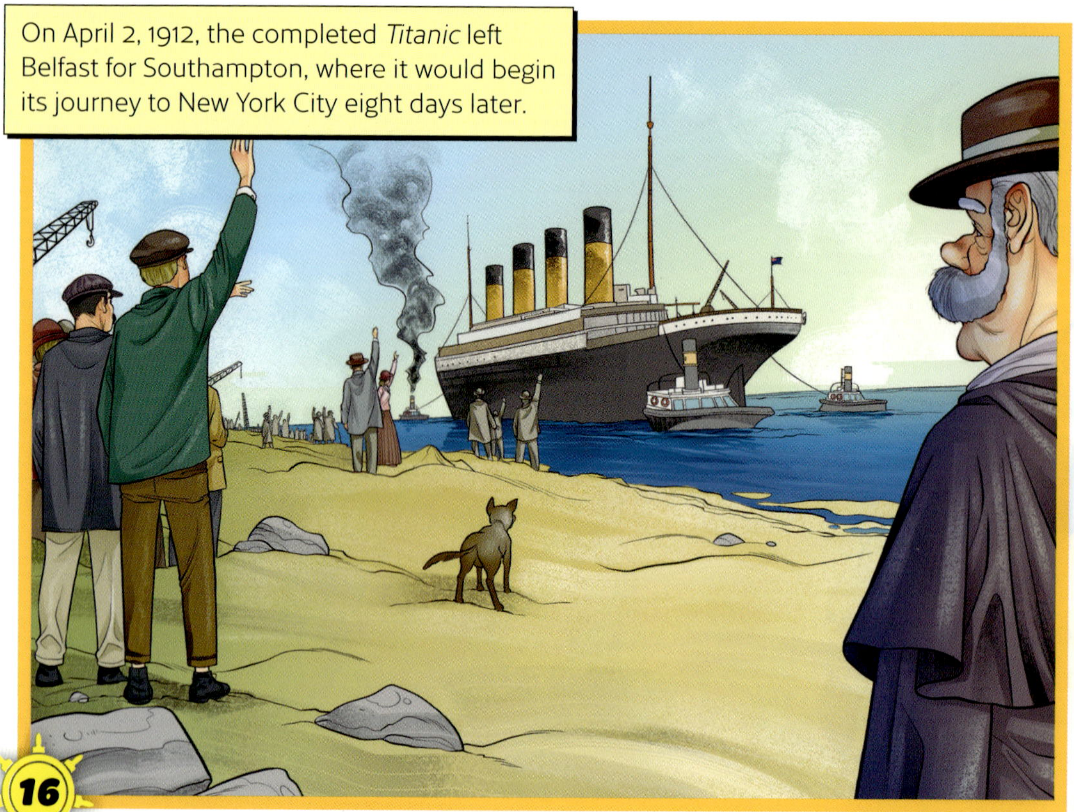
On April 2, 1912, the completed *Titanic* left Belfast for Southampton, where it would begin its journey to New York City eight days later.

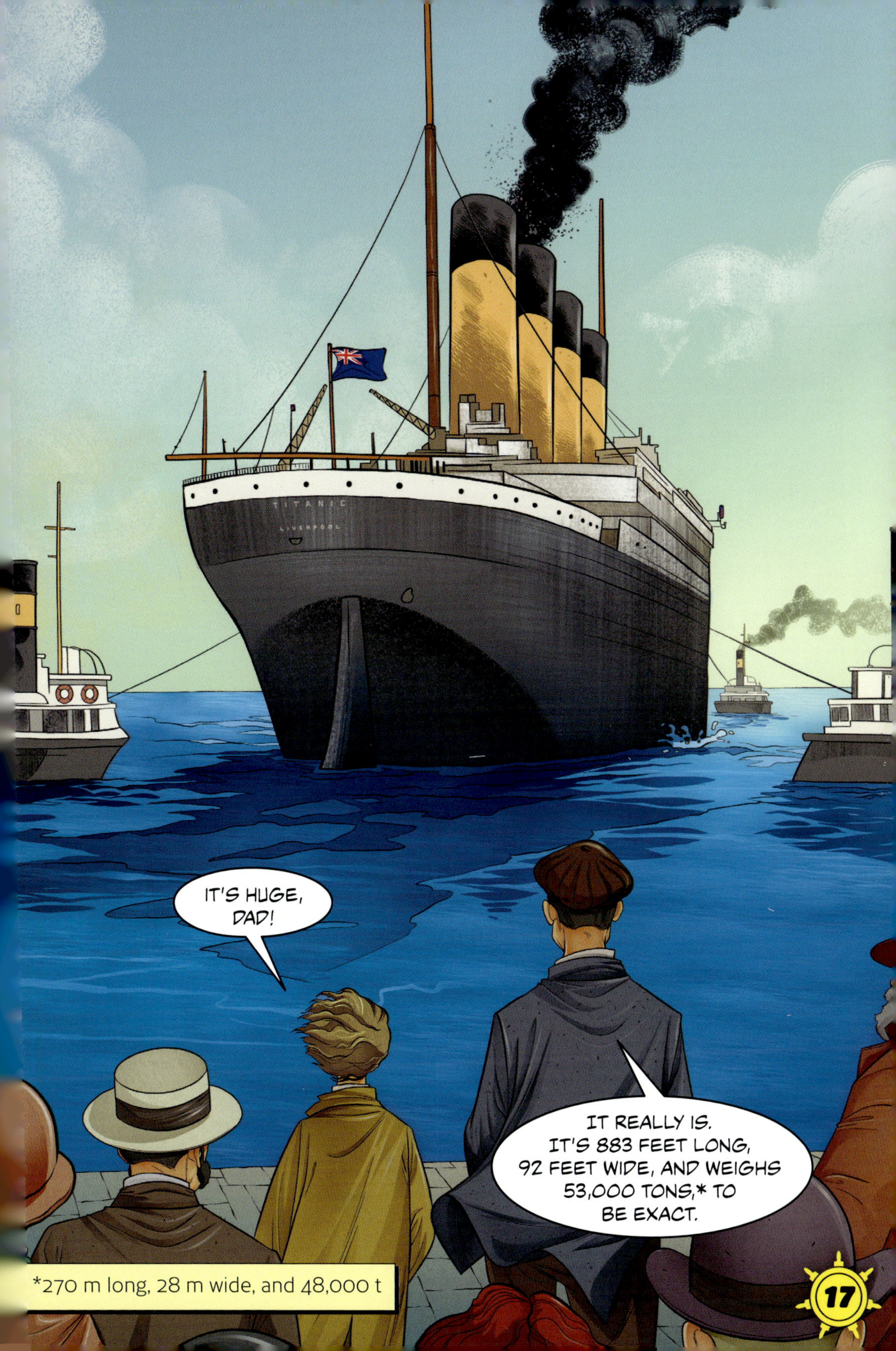
IT'S HUGE, DAD!
IT REALLY IS. IT'S 883 FEET LONG, 92 FEET WIDE, AND WEIGHS 53,000 TONS,* TO BE EXACT.
*270 m long, 28 m wide, and 48,000 t

CHAPTER 4

Fateful Voyage

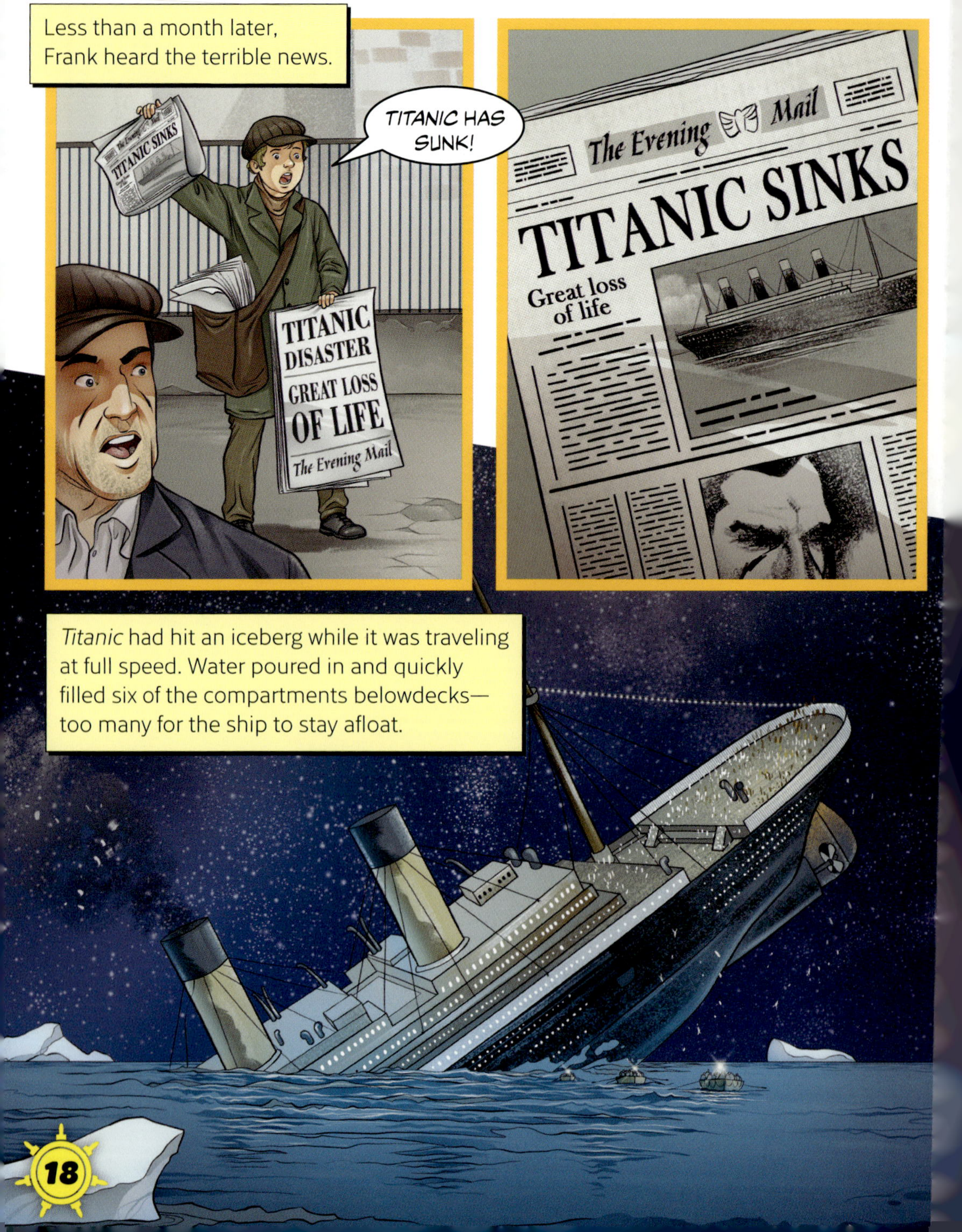
Less than a month later, Frank heard the terrible news.
TITANIC SINKS
TITANIC HAS SUNK!
TITANIC DISASTER
GREAT LOSS OF LIFE
The Evening Mail
The Evening Mail
TITANIC SINKS
Great loss of life
Titanic had hit an iceberg while it was traveling at full speed. Water poured in and quickly filled six of the compartments belowdecks—too many for the ship to stay afloat.

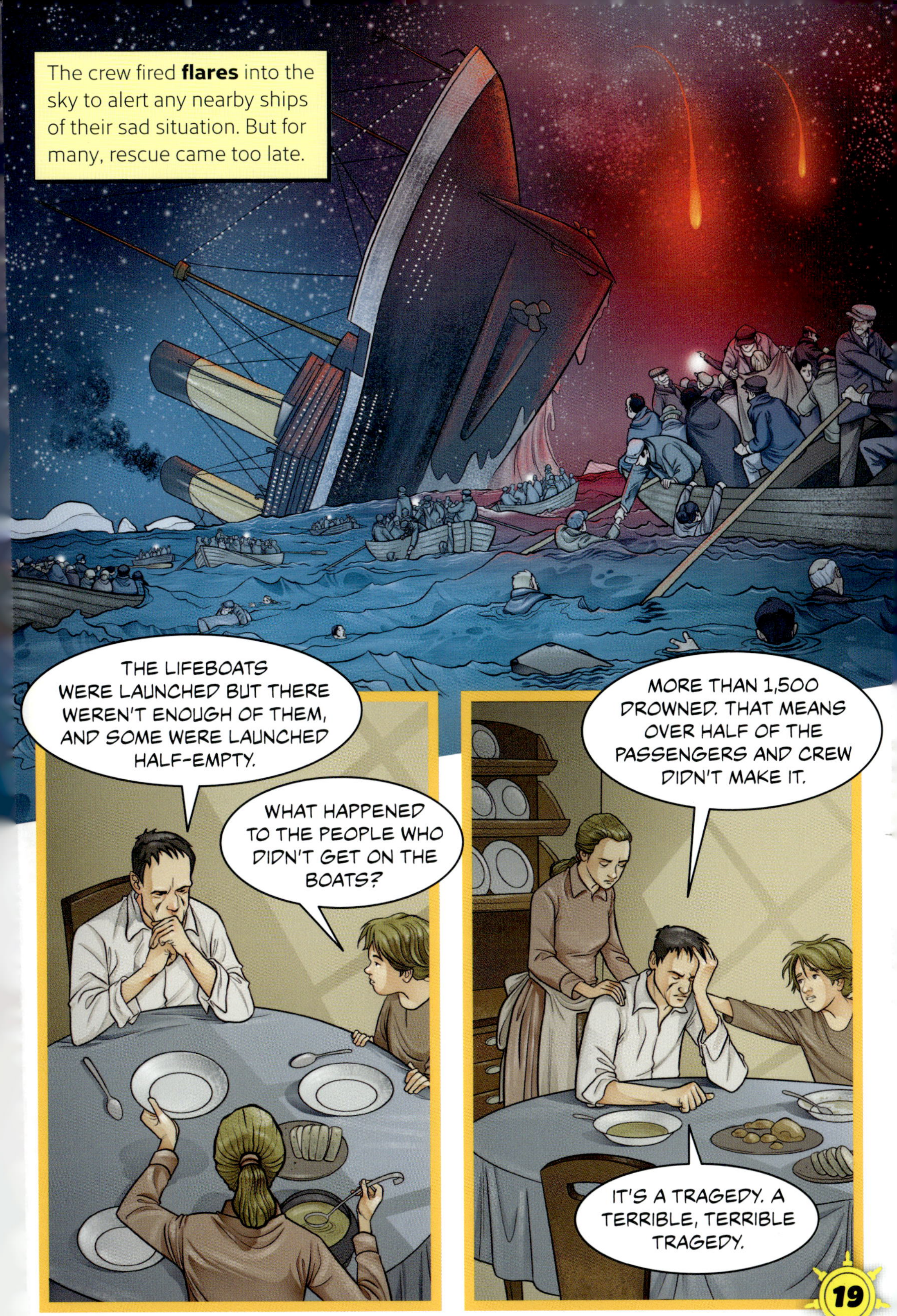
The crew fired **flares** into the sky to alert any nearby ships of their sad situation. But for many, rescue came too late.
THE LIFEBOATS WERE LAUNCHED BUT THERE WEREN'T ENOUGH OF THEM, AND SOME WERE LAUNCHED HALF-EMPTY.
WHAT HAPPENED TO THE PEOPLE WHO DIDN'T GET ON THE BOATS?
MORE THAN 1,500 DROWNED. THAT MEANS OVER HALF OF THE PASSENGERS AND CREW DIDN'T MAKE IT.
IT'S A TRAGEDY. A TERRIBLE, TERRIBLE TRAGEDY.

Life aboard *Titanic*

J. Bruce Ismay's dream was to create a ship like no other. In the 1900s, there was a growing demand for sea crossings—for business and vacation travel as well to take **immigrants** across the ocean to seek a better life abroad. The *Titanic* wasn't the fastest ship ever built, but it was designed to be the biggest and the best. It offered a five-day voyage from Southampton, England, to New York City. For the wealthiest passengers, the ship's facilities were outstanding.

First-class accommodations were found on the upper decks. Like a luxury hotel, these cabins were elegantly furnished and had multiple rooms and private bathrooms. First-class passengers enjoyed fine restaurants, a heated swimming pool, a spa, a barber shop, and even a squash court.

TITANIC'S FIRST-CLASS PASSENGERS ALSO HAD ACCESS TO A GYMNASIUM.

Second-class passengers were still treated to many luxuries, including a library, barbershop, and dining room. But for those in steerage, there was far less. More than 700 third-class passengers had to share tight quarters. These passengers slept in bunk rooms and didn't enjoy any of *Titanic*'s luxury features.

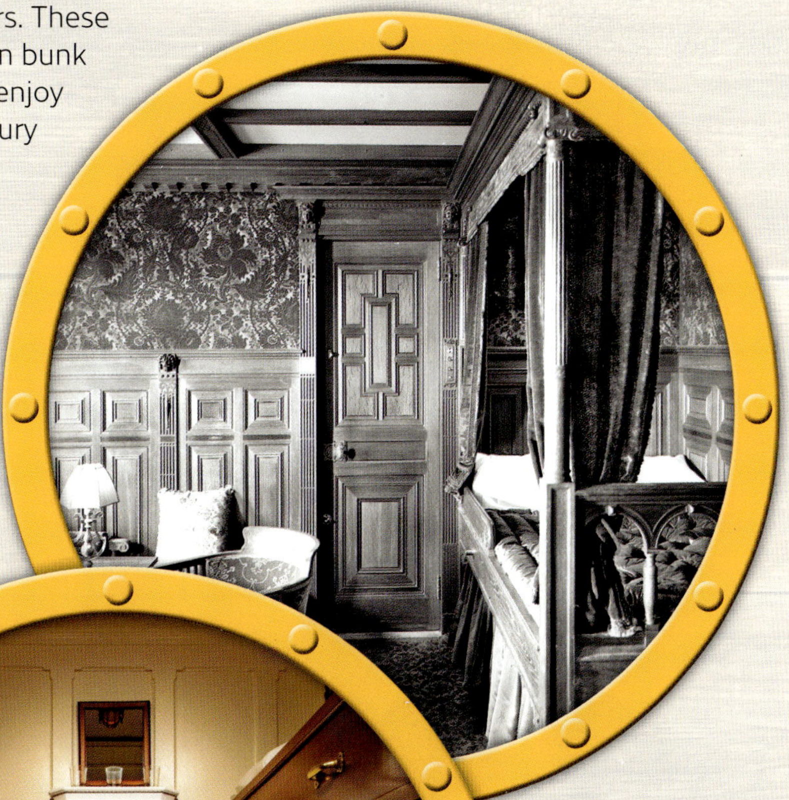

A FIRST-CLASS STATEROOM

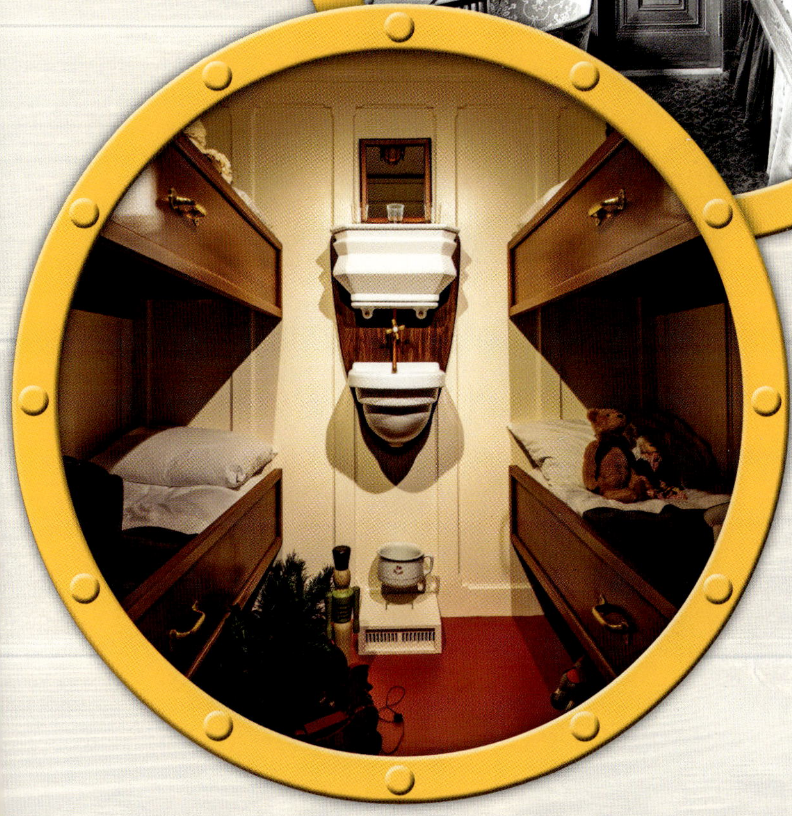

A REPLICA OF A THIRD-CLASS CABIN

More *Titanic* Stories

The *Titanic* was the vision of J. Bruce Ismay, the head of the British shipping company White Star Line. Prioritizing luxury over safety, Ismay approved installing fewer lifeboats in order to give first-class passengers a better view. He joined *Titanic*'s first voyage and was the highest-ranking official to survive. After the crash, Ismay reportedly helped women and children onto lifeboats first, and then he climbed into the last boat himself. This decision affected him the rest of his life. The press called Ismay a coward, and his reputation was shattered.

J. BRUCE ISMAY

THOMAS ANDREWS

Thomas Andrews, the ship's architect, also made a point of joining *Titanic*'s first—and ultimately only— voyage. During the trip, he made many notes on how the ship could be improved. When the *Titanic* struck the iceberg, Andrews checked his drawings and predicted that the ship would sink in less than two hours. He urged many women and children to board the lifeboats, saving lives as a result. Andrews sank with the ship and was later called a hero.

Glossary

ambitious wanting to reach a goal that may not be easy to achieve

bulkheads walls in a ship's hull that create watertight compartments

carpenters workers who build or repair wooden structures

construction the building of something, such as a building or a boat

cranes tall machines used to lift heavy objects

flares rockets fired into the sky to attract attention

hull the main body of a ship, including the bottom, sides, and deck

immigrants people who come to a country to permanently live there

luxuries expensive items or services that are desirable but not essential

marvel a wonderful or astonishing thing

opulent showing great wealth or expense

riveters workers who fasten things with metal pins known as rivets

slipways slopes leading down for boats to enter the water

FOR A TIME, THOMAS ANDREWS WAS HEAD OF THE DRAFTING DEPARTMENT OF THE SHIPBUILDING COMPANY HARLAND AND WOLFF.

23

Index

Read More

Crestodina, Tom. *Working Boats: An Inside Look at Ten Amazing Watercraft.* Seattle: Sasquatch Books, 2022.

Enz, Tammy. *Science on the* Titanic *(The Science of History).* North Mankato, MN: Capstone Press, 2023.

Shepherd, Jodie. *Building the* Titanic *(A True Book: The* Titanic*).* Danbury, CT: Children's Press, 2022.

Learn More Online

1. Go to **FactSurfer.com** or scan the QR code below.
2. Enter "**Building Ship of Dreams**" into the search box.
3. Click on the cover of this book to see a list of websites.